Praying
the
Psalms

Praying
the
Psalms

**Walter
Brueggemann**

**Saint Mary's Press
Christian Brothers Publications
Winona, Minnesota**

The scriptural citations in this publication are from the New Revised Standard Version of the Bible. Copyright © 1989 by the Division of Christian Education of the National Council of the Churches of Christ in the U.S.A. Used by permission. All rights reserved. Italics added to some quotations for emphasis.

Photo credits: Cover, pages 8, 12, Gail Denham; page 22, Rohn Engh Photography; page 56, Jean-Claude Lejeune; pages 32, 42, Richard T. Nowitz.

The publishing team included Carl Koch, FSC, development editor; Joellen Barak, manuscript editor; Amy Schlumpf Manion, typesetter; Maura C. Goessling, cover designer; pre-press, printing, and binding by the graphics division of Saint Mary's Press.

Printed in the United States of America

Printing: 9 8 7 6 5 4 3 2 1

Year: 2001 00 99 98 97 96 95 94 93

Library of Congress card catalog number 81-86045

ISBN 0-88489-322-7

For

Lila Bonner Miller

Contents

Preface

Psalm study among scholars has been on something of a plateau for some time. The dominant positions of Hermann Gunkel on form-critical matters and Sigmund Mowinckel on cultic context are still in place. Beyond their brilliant proposals, there has been little movement that would link scholarly work to the life of the Psalms in the church.

Important contributions have been made in developing the connections between scholarship and church. Among the most significant of these are Bernhard Anderson's *Out of the Depths* (Philadelphia: Westminster Press, 1974) and Claus Westermann's *The Psalms: Structure, Content and Message* (Minneapolis: Augsburg Press, 1980). More popularly, see also Thomas H. Troeger's *Rage! Reflect, Rejoice!* (Philadelphia: Westminster Press, 1977). And there is more to come out of the fertile suggestions of Rainer Albertz and Erhard Gerstenberger, whose works await translation.

This book does not attempt to go over the consensus of scholarship again. Rather than repeat so much material, here the work of Gunkel and Mowinckel is assumed. Nor do we need to review the extensive secondary material derived from that consensus. This book attempts to address only two specific issues, which hopefully will aid in reading the Psalms both more knowingly and more passionately.

The first issue concerns the function of *language* in the use of the Psalms. It is clear that conventional exegesis will not make contact with the compelling power of the poetry of the Psalms. And, in large part, this failure of language causes the gap between the scholarly consensus and the vast array of "devotional materials." Here, I have not spent time on the foundations of linguistic function to which I appeal. I have tried to show how the Psalms might be liberated for more poignant and faithful use if we will grant to the language of the Psalms the imaginative and free play that must have been intended. I claim no expertise on linguistic theory, but it will be evident that I have found the work of Paul Ricoeur most helpful and stimulating. A more comprehensive statement of my presuppositions and my use of Ricoeur's work is given in "Psalms and the Life of Faith: A Suggested Typology of Function," *Journal for the Study of the Old Testament* 17 (1980): 3–32.

The second issue considered is the Christian use of *poetry that is obviously Jewish*. It is clear that the next efforts in Christian theology must concern interaction with Jewish faith. Undoubtedly Jewish faith is problematic for Christians. Concerning the Psalms, Christians (in practice if not in theory) deal with the Jewish "awkwardness" either by cunning selectivity or by knowing spiritualization. Either way, such use misses the point. It is of course hazardous for a Christian to make a statement about the Jewishness in these texts. I have taken a risk about that and perhaps have not done it rightly. But I hope my statement, if it is enough on target, may contribute to the urgent interface of Christian worship and Jewish faith. Even if my statement is not right, I hope it is clear that I have acted in good faith.

On both the question of the liberation of language and the question of Jewish awkwardness, very much is at stake for the church. I hope to contribute to the vitality of the church's faith by pointing to the subversive and powerful resources available in the Psalms. It is an unreformed church that uses the Psalms for a domesticated spirituality. It is not an accident that the Reformers of the sixteenth century attended to the Psalms in intensive ways. On both questions taken up, I have reference to "the one from whom no secret can be hid." On the one hand, I have urged that language here is not only for candor but for the articulation of that which is known—both by God and by human persons— only when articulated. Everything depends on the articulation, for such speech evokes something quite new for both parties in the conversation. That no secret can be hidden depends on such risky articulation.

On the other hand, I have argued that such candor is not an empty, neutral form but has a distinctively Jewish shape—the shape of active, protesting suffering; the shape of defiant, resilient hope. The *stuff* of Jewish suffering and Jewish hope is a unique partner to the *form* of strident, subversive, intense language. That is, this bold form of speech peculiarly matches the Jewish practice of suffering and hope. It is the interplay of the *stuff of Jewish faith* and the *form of psalmic speech* that might matter to the spirituality of the church.

I should say a word about how this little book came to be. It is as spotty and selective as it is because it was originally a series of separately printed papers. They were written at the behest of the late Mary Perkins Ryan, who had them published in *Professional Approaches for Christian Educators (PACE)* by Saint Mary's Press. The pieces were not intended to be comprehensive or complete; they are only suggestions for along the way in reading and praying the Psalms. I have intended that these suggestions should be not only exegetical, but hermeneutical as well. Mary Perkins Ryan was a strong and supportive editor. If these papers do not quite amount to a well-argued book, their original intent and purpose must be kept in mind.

We have decided to use the New Revised Standard Version of the Bible because it probably is the most widely used among readers of this book. Unless stated otherwise, our references are to the NRSV.

The dedication is to Lila Bonner Miller, MD. She combines in her life and her psychotherapeutic practice all the abrasive candor of liberated faith and all the certitude of unflinching trust that belongs to this tradition. She was formed in the Psalms in the practice of the Associate Reformed Presbyterian church. Not only has she remained in that nurture, but she has also practiced the Psalms in bold ways, with both her spirit and her mind (1 Cor. 14:15). That is a great gift to many persons, including this son-in-law.

1

Letting Experience Touch the Psalter

We pray together regularly "for all sorts and conditions of men" (and women), as the Book of Common Prayer puts it. We know all about these sorts and conditions, for we are among and like all those others. When we pray for them, we pray for ourselves. We are able to pray for others precisely because we share a "common lot." They are like us, and we are like them in decisive ways. Thus one way to know about "all sorts and conditions of men" and women is to be attentive to what is happening in our own life.

A second way in which we know about others is by being attentive to what is written—in the daily newspaper as well as in great literature. The daily newspaper is a summary and a chronicle of what goes on among us; the healings and betrayals, the power sought and gained, the brokenness and gifts and victories. All of that belongs to these "sorts and conditions" for whom we pray.

In addition to our own experience and the testimonies of print, the Psalms of the Hebrew Scriptures offer a third presentation of how it is with all "sorts and conditions of men" and women. The Psalms, with a few exceptions, are not the voice of God addressing us. They are rather the voice of our own common humanity, gathered over a long period of time; a voice that continues to have amazing authenticity and contemporaneity. It speaks about life the way it really is, for the same issues and possibilities persist in those deeply human dimensions. And so when we turn to the Psalms, it means we enter into that voice of humanity and decide to take our stand with that voice. We are prepared to speak among all people and with them and for them, to express our solidarity in this anguished, joyous, human pilgrimage. We add a voice to the common elation, shared grief, and communal rage that beset us all.

In order to pray the Psalms, our work (liturgy is indeed work) is to let our voice and mind and heart run back and forth in regular and speedy interplay between the stylized and sometimes too familiar words of the *Scriptures,* and our *experience,* which we sense with poignancy. And when we do, we shall find that the words of the Scriptures bring power, shape, and authority to what we know about ourselves. Conversely, our experience brings to the words of the Scriptures an immediacy and a vitality that must always be reasserted within the Psalter.

Beyond Our Time of Equilibrium

Before turning to the Psalms, let us consider the "sorts and conditions" that are true of all of us and that come to speech in the Psalms. I suggest, in a simple schematic fashion, that our life of faith consists in moving with God in terms of

   a. being securely *oriented*,
   b. being painfully *disoriented*, and
   c. being surprisingly *reoriented*.

This general way of speaking can apply to our self-acceptance, our relations to significant others, and our participation in public issues. It can permit us to speak of passages, the life cycle, stages of growth, and identity crises. It can permit us to be honest about what is happening to us. Most of all, it may provide us with a way to think about the Psalms in relation to our common human experience, for each of God's children is in transit along the flow of orientation, disorientation, and reorientation.

The first situation in this scheme, that of being securely oriented, is one of equilibrium. While we all yearn for it, it is not very interesting, and it does not produce great prayer or powerful song. It consists in being well settled, knowing that life makes sense and that God is well placed in heaven, presiding but not bothering. This is the mood of much of the middle-class church. In terms of the Bible, this attitude of equilibrium and safe orientation is best reflected in the teaching of the old Proverbs, which affirm that life is equitable, symmetrical, and well proportioned. This mood of humanness is minimal in the Psalms but may be reflected in Psalm 37, which is mostly a collection of sayings that could just as well be placed in Proverbs. The same is more eloquently reflected in such a marvelous statement as Psalm 145, which trusts everything to God. Such psalms reflect confident well-being. In order to pray them, we must locate, either in our life or in the life of others, situations of such confident, buoyant, "successful" living.

But that is a minor theme in the Psalms and not very provocative. The Psalms mostly do not emerge out of such situations of equilibrium. Rather, people are driven to the Psalter's poignant prayer and song precisely by *experiences of dislocation and relocation*. It is experiences of being overwhelmed, nearly destroyed, and then surprisingly given life that empower us to pray and sing.

In the Rawness of Life

Recently there has been considerable discussion of those events that drive us to the edge of humanness and make us peculiarly open to the Holy One. This investigation, pertinent to our theme, is undertaken because many persons conclude that the "religious dimension" of their life is void. And so they ask about those elements in life that relate to the "hunger for transcendence." In a variety of ways, it is suggested that the events at the edge of our humanness, the events that threaten and disrupt our convenient equilibrium, are the same ones that may fill us with passion and evoke eloquence in us. Thus, the Psalms reflect such passionate and eloquent events that occur when experience presses us to address the Holy One.

We have noted the convergence of our experience, the newspaper accounts, and the Psalms as being articulations of our deep human experience. But we should distinguish the Psalms in one important point. Unlike our own experience and that of the newspaper, it is the Psalms that present "all sorts and conditions of men" and women addressed to the Holy God. Thus the events at the edge of humanness, which are so crucial for us and which are reflected in the Psalms, tend to

    a. evoke *eloquence,*
    b. fill us with *passion,* and
    c. turn us to the *Holy One.*

As we enter into the prayer and song of common humanity in the Psalms, it is helpful to be attentive precisely to the simple eloquence, the overriding passion, and the bold ways in which this common voice turns to the Holy One.

What situations drive us to the edge of our humanness? They are situations of extremity for which conventional equilibrium offers no adequate base. Peter Berger[1] refers to these extremities as experiences that are filled with "a rumor of angels," a hint of some surplus of meaning. He suggests that they include experiences of order, play, hope, damnation, and humor.

Langdon Gilkey[2] speaks of experiences of "contingency," when we become aware of how precarious our life is, and aware also of the inexplicable givenness of it. For Gilkey, these dimensions include experiences of givenness, threat, limitedness, value, freedom, and condemnation. Following Karl Jaspers, Paul Ricoeur refers to "limit-experiences"—death, suffering, guilt, and hatred—and also to "'peak experiences,' especially experiences of creation and joy which are no less extreme than are experiences of catastrophe."[3] Reference to Berger, Gilkey, and Ricoeur tells us something important about prayer, especially in the Psalms. Reflect for a moment on the coined phrases of "a rumor of angels," "the whirlwind," "contingency," "limit-experiences." In different ways, all three writers—a sociologist, a theologian, and a philosopher interested in psychology—are pointing to the deep discontinuities in our life, on which we use most of our energies, and about which we are regularly preoccupied.

Thus we follow Berger, Gilkey, and Ricoeur in suggesting that the experiences of life that lie beyond our conventional copings are those which make us eloquent and passionate and which drive us to speak to the Holy One. And it is experiences beyond conventional orientations that come to vivid expression in the Psalms. That is what we mean by "all sorts and conditions of men" and women—that we are dealing here with the powerful, dangerous, and joyful rawness of human reality. In the Psalms, we find the voice that dares to speak of these matters with eloquence and passion to the Holy One. The Psalms offer speech when life has gone beyond our frail efforts to control it.[4]

The Psalms thus propose to speak about human experience in an honest, freeing way. This is in contrast to much of human speech and conduct, which is in fact a cover-up. In most of life's arenas, we are expected and required to speak the language of safe orientation and equilibrium, either to find life so or to pretend we find it so. For the normal, conventional functioning of public life, the raw edges of disorientation and reorientation must be either denied or suppressed for purposes of public equilibrium. As a result, our speech is dulled and mundane. Our passion has been stilled and is without imagination. Often the Holy One is not addressed, not because we dare not, but because God is far away and hardly seems important. Therefore, the agenda and intention of the Psalms are considerably at odds with the normal speech of most people—the normal speech of a stable, functioning, self-deceptive culture in which everything must be kept young and running smoothly.

Against that, the speech of the Psalms is abrasive, revolutionary, and dangerous. It announces that our common experience is not one of well-being and equilibrium, that life is not like that. Life is instead a churning, disruptive experience of dislocation and relocation. Perhaps in our conventional, routinized prayer life (e.g., the daily practice of the office) that is one of the reasons the Psalter does not yield its power—because out of habit or fatigue or numbness, we try to use the Psalms in our equilibrium. When we do that, we miss the point of the Psalms. Moreover, our own experience may be left untapped and inarticulate and, therefore, not liberated. Such surface use of the Psalms coincides with the denial of the discontinuities in our own experience. Ernest Becker has written of *The Denial of Death*.[5] But such denial happens not just at crisis points. It happens daily in the reduction of language to numb conventions.

Thus I suggest that most of the Psalms can only be appropriately prayed by people who are living at the edges of their life, sensitive to the raw hurts, the primitive passions, and the naive elations that are at the bottom of life. For most of us, liturgical or devotional entry into the Psalms requires a real change of pace. It asks us to depart from the closely managed world of public survival, to move into the open, frightening, healing world of speech with the Holy One.

Lament as Speeches of Disorientation

So let us consider in turn the experiences of *disorientation* and *reorientation* which characterize human life and which are the driving power of the Psalms. If we move from the premise of equilibrium, we may speak of *chaos* (disorder) and *new order.* These are elemental dimensions, both to our experience and to the Psalms. The Psalms, by and large, emerge from and reflect precisely such situations of chaos and new order. Any attempt to make these speech-events of chaos and new order into instruments of conventional equilibrium is a travesty. To make the Psalms serve "business as usual" misunderstands the Psalms, and habitual use of them has tended to do just that.

So first, the reality of chaos, disorder, disorientation: Each of us knows about that in our own life. It may be a visible issue like a marriage failure, the loss of a job, a financial reverse, the diagnosis of the doctor. It may be nothing more than a cross word, a disappointing letter, a sharp criticism, a minor illness. Or it may be disturbance of a public kind, anxiety over the loss of energy, revulsion at the sickening spectacle of war, the sense that the world is falling apart before our very eyes, the unspeakable horror of a possible nuclear war. It may be the discovery of loneliness, the sense of being rejected and unloved. All or any of these trigger the awareness that life is not whole, that it is not the romantic well-being which we were taught in Sunday school, and which is so shamefully and shrewdly reflected in television ads. Indeed the world is a dangerous, frightening place, and I am upset for myself. And when I can move beyond my own fear and grief, I do not need to look far to find the hurt and terror others have, whether these others are my own friends or people I see and hear about on television.

The Psalter knows that life is dislocated. There need be no cover-up. The Psalter is a collection of the eloquent, passionate songs and prayers of people who are at the desperate edges of their life. The stylized form of such speech is the lament psalm, of which there are many examples. The best known is Psalm 22. The neatest, simplest example is Psalm 13. The angriest, most hopeless is Psalm 88, which ends in unreserved, unrelieved gloom.

Thus I propose a direct link between the experience of dislocation in which we all share and the lament psalm of Israel.

There are those who know about disorientation but have no speech that can adequately reflect it. But there are also those (and this is our primary concern here) who face the lament psalm but do not bring to it the raw disorientation which is all about us, and which is the intended agenda of the psalm. It is the work of the one who prays a psalm to be actively engaged in holding this linkage in a conscious, concrete way. For when we do, we discover that the psalm is affected by our experience, and, even more surprising, we find that our experience has been dealt with by the psalm.

We must not make these psalms too "religious" or pious. Most of the lament psalms are the voices of those who "are mad as hell and are not going to take it any more." They are not religious in the sense that they are courteous or polite or deferential. They are religious only in the sense that they are willing to speak this chaos to the very face of the Holy One. Thus the lament psalm, for all its preoccupation with the hard issues at hand, invariably calls God by name and expects a response. At this crucial point, the psalm parts company with our newspaper evidence and most of our experience, for it is disorientation *addressed to God.* And in that address, something happens to the disorientation.

The Surprising Songs of Newness

The other movement of human life is the surprising move from disorientation to a new orientation that is quite unlike the old status quo. This is not an automatic movement that can be presumed or predicted. Nor is it a return to the old form, a return to normalcy as though nothing had happened. It is rather "all things new." When it happens, it is always a surprise, always a gift of graciousness, and always an experience that evokes gratitude. It may be thought that in our daily experience, the events of reorientation are not as frequent as the times of dislocation. Perhaps that is so. Perhaps we have not learned to discern the ways the wondrous gift is given. We dare to say that in our existence there is the richness of life along with the reality of death. There is the power of resurrection as well as the inescapability of crucifixion. The conquest of chaos and the gift of fresh life-giving order must also be brought to speech. Such experiences include all those gifts of friendship and caring, all those gestures of reconciliation and forgiveness, all those risky signs of hope in public life, all experiences that may touch us deeply and announce that God has not left the world to chaos (cf. Isa. 45:18–19).

We may not notice these events unless we practice the language of praise and thanks. For this, the Psalter offers us the celebrative language of hymns and songs of thanksgiving,[6] which sometimes assert the abiding rule of God (as in Psalm 103), but at other times announce the surprising intrusion of God who just now makes things good (Psalm 114). This is what is meant in the psalms that announce "The LORD is King" (Pss. 96:10; 97:1; 98:6; 99:1). They celebrate some experience that has brought the speaker's world to a new and joyous orientation. Thus I suggest that there is a linkage to be maintained between the *experiences of reorientation* and Israel's *psalms and hymns of thanksgiving*. There are those who have a sense of the new gift of life and, lamentably, have no way to speak about it. But there are also those (and this is our primary concern here) who have regular access to the psalms of high celebration, but have been so numbed to their own experience that the words of the Psalms have no counterpart in their own life experience.

The collection of the Psalter is not for those whose life is one of uninterrupted continuity and equilibrium. Such people should stay safely in the Book of Proverbs, which reflects on the continuities of life. But few live that kind of life. Most of us who think we do have actually been numbed, desensitized, and suppressed, and we are cut off from what is in fact going on in our life.

The Psalms are an assurance to us that when we pray and worship, we are not expected to censure or deny the deepness of our own human pilgrimage. Rather, we are expected to submit it openly and trustingly so that it can be brought to eloquent and passionate speech addressed to the Holy One. If we are genuinely attentive to these linkages of speech and experience, we discover that we pray a prayer along with our brothers and sisters, who may be in very different circumstances. Others may give a different nuance to their speech, but they also have the realities of disorientation and reorientation in their lives. Thus they join in this resilient voice addressed to the Holy One. The Psalms are not used in a vacuum but in a history where we are dying and rising, and in a history where God is at work, ending our life and making a gracious new beginning for us. The Psalms move with our experience. They may also take us beyond our own guarded experience into the more poignant pilgrimages of sisters and brothers.

2

The Liberation
of Language

Praying the Psalms depends upon two things: (1) what we *find* there when we come to the Psalms and (2) what we *bring* to the Psalms out of our own life. In our first chapter, we have urged that when we come to the Psalms we shall *find* their eloquence and passion and boldness in addressing the Holy One. Further, we have urged that what we *bring* to the Psalter in order to pray is a candid openness to the extremities in our own life and in the life of others. These extremities recognize the depths of despair and death; they acknowledge the sheer gift of life.

The work of prayer is to bring these two realities together— the boldness of the Psalms and the extremity of our experience—to let them interact, play with each other, tease each other, and illuminate each other. The work of prayer consists in the imaginative use of language to give the extremities their full due and to force new awareness and new configurations of reality by the boldness of our speech. All this is to submit to the Holy One in order that we may be addressed by a Word that out-distances all our speech.

A Language Adequate to Experience

Let us begin with a presupposition about language that is necessary to enter into the Psalms. In our culture, we imbibe a positivistic understanding of language. That is, we believe that the function of language is only to report and describe what already exists. The usefulness of such language is obvious. It lets us be precise and unambiguous. It even lets us control. But it is one-dimensional language that must necessarily be without passion, and without eloquence, and indeed without boldness. It is useful language, but it is not the language we have in the Psalms. Indeed, it is not the language in which we can faithfully pray. Such language is useful for managing things. But it makes no impact on how things really are, for things would be the same even if there were no such speech.

In the Psalms, the use of language does not *describe* what is. It takes what has not yet been spoken and *evokes* it into being. This kind of speech resists discipline, shuns precision, delights in ambiguity, is profoundly creative, and is itself an exercise in freedom. In using speech in this way, we are in fact doing on a smaller scale what God has done in the Creation narratives of Genesis. We are calling into being that which does not yet exist (cf. Rom. 4:17).

Now in contrasting these two kinds of language, we need to be clear about the social function of each. The first mode of language is appropriate to science, engineering, and perhaps the social sciences. When it is used in the arena of human interaction, however, it tends to be conservative, restrictive, and limiting. It can only describe what already exists and, by its very use, deter anything new from coming into being. It crushes hope, for it cannot "imagine" what is not already present. By contrast, the bold, symbolic use of language in the Psalms is restive with what *is*. It races on ahead to form something that never was before. This language, then, with its speech of liberation, is dangerous and revolutionary, for its very use constitutes a threat to the way things have been. It is for this reason that totalitarian regimes, even when they control all the hardware, are most fearful of the poet. The creative speech of the poet can evoke new forms of human life that even the power of arms and repression is helpless to prevent. Such speech, which is the proper idiom for prayer, is the language of surprise. It means that in such speech both the speaker and God may be surprised by what is freshly offered. The language of the Psalms permits us to be boldly *anticipatory* about what may be, as well as *discerning* about what has been.

A great danger in praying the Psalms is that we shall mistakenly take their language in a positivistic, descriptive way as nothing more than a report on what is. Taken that way, the Psalms can probably be managed, comprehended, and rendered powerless. That is a hazard of the repeated use of any important words. We assume we already know what they mean. But if the language of the Psalms is understood impressionistically and creatively, then it holds surprise and in fact creates new realities where none existed before.

Lament as Candor and Anticipation

Let us consider the function and power of such speech with reference to the two kinds of psalms we identified in chapter one. First, we said that *psalms of lament are powerful expressions of the experience of disorientation.* They express the pain, grief, dismay, and anger that life is not good. (They also refuse to settle for things as they are, and so they assert hope.) One of the things to notice is that these psalms engage in enormous hyperbole. Thus:

> I am poured out like water,
>   and all my bones are out of joint;
> my heart is like wax . . .
> my mouth is dried up like a potsherd. . . .
>
> (22:14-15)

> . . . Every night I flood my bed with tears;
>   I drench my couch with my weeping.
>
> (6:6)

> My tears have been my food day and night. . . .
>
> (42:3; cf. Isa. 16:9)

> My enemies trample upon me all day long. . . .
>
> (56:2)

> I lie down among lions. . . .
>
> (57:4)

What are we to make of this? If this is descriptive speech, we may take it as likely that not every bone is out of joint, that not the whole bed is drenched, that there must have been other meat, that the speaker has not been trampled all day, for that happens only in TV wrestling. If it is descriptive, we must conclude that the speech is irrelevant, because it resembles no experience of our own. But this is not descriptive language. It is evocative language used to create between speaker and God something that did not fully exist before; namely, a total, publicly acknowledged event of dislocation and disorientation. With this speech, the dislocation becomes a visible event that now exists between the pray-er and God. With this portrayal, God is compelled to notice. We now know, of course, that at the time of death, the healthy grief process requires many tears, many words, many embraces, many retellings of the grief. It is so for every extremity of dislocation. This is indeed grief *work,* and we are invited to join in it.

The function of such lament speech is to create a situation that did not exist before the speech, to create an external event that matches the internal sensitivities. It is the work of such speech to give shape, power, visibility, authenticity, to the experience. The speaker now says, "That is my situation. It is really like that." The listener knows, "Now I understand fully your actual situation. You are working to die to the old equilibrium that is slipping from you." The language may even run ahead of the event. Ricoeur[1] (to whom much of this discussion is indebted), following Freud, states that the authentic artist does not focus on reviewing old events (after the manner of the analyst), but in fact commits an act of hope. Art therapists know that persons who draw and paint are not simply announcing the old death but are choosing a future they are yet to embrace. Thus the lament psalms of disorientation help people to die completely to the old situation—the old possibility, the old false hopes, the old lines of defense and pretense—to say as dramatically as possible, "That is all over now."

When we hear someone speak desperately about a situation, our wont is to rush in and reassure that it is not all that bad. And in hearing these psalms, our natural, fearful yearning is to tone down the hyperbole, to deny it for ourselves and protect others from it because it is too harsh and, in any case, is an overstatement. We wish to hold on a bit to the old orientation, now in such disarray. Our tendency to such protectiveness is evident in the way churches ignore or "edit" these "unacceptable" psalms.

Our retreat from the poignant language of such a psalm is in fact a denial of the disorientation and a yearning to hold on to the old orientation that is, in reality, dead. Thus an evangelical understanding of reality affirms that the old is passing away, that God is bringing in a newness (2 Cor. 5:17). But we know also that there is no newness unless and until there is a serious death of the old (cf. John 12:25; 1 Cor. 15:36). Thus the lament psalms of disorientation can be understood, not theoretically but in a quite concrete way, as an act of putting off the old humanity so that the new may come (cf. Eph. 4:22-24).

So, how to pray these psalms? I suggest that praying them requires the location of experiences in our own life and in the life of others when inclinations and realities of disorientation were singing among us. The bed full of tears, the body full of disconnectedness, the plate full of salty tears, the day full of trampling—these are events not remote from us. In our disciplined, restrained ways of managing, we may be too uptight to cry. We may be too dulled to feel the trampling or to acknowledge it. But we do know what it feels like to be kicked when we are down. How wondrous that these psalms make it clear that precisely such dimensions of our life are the stuff of prayer. The psalms thus become a voice for the dying in which we are all engaged, partly because the world is a place of death and is passing away, partly because God gives new life, but only in the pain of death. It is because God is at work even in the pain of such death that the psalmist dares enter God's presence with these realities. They have to do with God.

Language Permitting Transformation

The celebrative psalms and hymns of thanksgiving powerfully express experiences of reorientation. Reorientation is always a surprise and a gift. It always comes to us just when we thought it not possible, when we could not see how it could be wrought in the present circumstance. The reorientation is not an achievement coming from us. It is not an automatic "next stage" ordained in our body, but it is something we receive when we did not expect it at all. Life falls into patterns of wholeness where we did not think reorientation could happen, precisely and only because God is at work.

Again, we shall see that the psalms of celebration also greatly overstate the case because they are essentially promissory. That is, they are not descriptions of what is evident, but they are renderings of what is surely promised and toward which the speaker is prepared to live. It may be urged, here more than in the psalms of lament, that these statements engage in fantasy and assert things that are not "in hand." Thus, for example, the key assertion of these psalms, "Yahweh is king," strikes one as ludicrous in our world, because most of the evidence of the newspapers suggests God is not in power. If the words of these psalms must be descriptive, then such a claim is deceptive, for God manifestly is not king. But if the words are evocative of a new reality yet to come, then the words have a powerful function. And indeed, sometimes in a world where the circumstances are hopeless, a promissory word is all that stands between us and the chaos. Then it is important to pray and speak and sing and share that word against all that data. For such a word stands like a barrier thrown up against the sea (cf. Jer. 5:22). We do know that in our most precious friendships, sometimes there is only a word between us and misery, between us and death. But that word is not a fantasy. It is, rather, a precious gift on which we will stake everything. Thus as the psalms of lament are acts of *painful relinquishment*,[2] so celebrative psalms are acts of *radical hope*.

In the psalms of celebration, we may consider three ways of speaking, which correlate to those we have cited in the laments.

First, songs of lament focus frequently on the threat of enemies seeking to destroy. Many of these psalms speak about *enemies*, even though they are not clearly identified. The responding assertion of celebration is that *Yahweh is king*, that God is graciously inclined and powerfully enthroned and that because of God's rule, the enemies are no threat. Most scholars agree that at least in Psalms 47, 93, 96–99, this is the central motif. In a less precise way, this is a main theme of every song of celebration: the triumphant rule of Yahweh against every agent who would diminish us. Those who pray this kind of psalm will want not just to reflect on a general notion of well-being but to work with the concrete image of king, the gracious ruler who does indeed manage well, protect the weak, intervene for the helpless, and provide for the people. To clarify, it may be useful to focus on situations in our own life when the simple presence of a trusted, respected person made a decisive difference. Or you may wish to reflect on the times of intervention when the kingship of Jesus totally redefined your situation (cf. Mark 3:1–6; 5:15,41–42; 6:41–44).

Second, we have commented on the *diet of tears* that belongs to the lament. In the songs of celebration, the metaphor of tears is perhaps balanced by the metaphor of food, of banquet, of a *bounteous table.* Of course, the best known of these is in Ps. 23:5, "You prepare a table before me in the presence of my enemies." For a terser style, see Ps. 146:7, which relates food to those who are hungry, and Ps. 147:9, food to the other creatures of the earth (cf. 81:10). An engagement of the metaphor of food is fundamental. There is no gesture as expressive of utter well-being as lavish food. Thus the feeding miracles of Jesus and the Eucharist are gestures of a new orientation, which comes as a surprising gift and ends all diets of tears.

Third, we have considered the metaphor of being *trampled* as a motif of disorientation. Notice that in being trampled, one is passive and acted upon. I suggest that in the songs of celebration, perhaps a counterpart of being trampled on is the act of *clapping,* of actively publicly engaging in a concrete gesture of commitment and reception of the new time. The clapping is to cheer the new king, that is, the new orientation, the arrival of the promised kingdom (Pss. 47:1; 98:8; cf. Isa. 55:12). Less concrete, but related to it, is the call to praise; so that in the later psalms (especially 148, but cf. 149:1–3,5–6), everything and everyone is mobilized to applaud, welcome, and receive. In praying these psalms, the one who prays may want to recall times in which there was some good news that had to be shared. Other people had to be recruited to celebrate and rejoice because the news was too good to keep to oneself (cf. Luke 15:6,9,23).

Poetry Requiring Work

So let me conclude with three comments. First, I have urged that the Psalms are filled with metaphors that need to be accepted *as metaphors* and not flattened into descriptive words. Metaphors are concrete words rooted in visible reality, but yet are enormously elastic, giving full play to imagination in stretching and extending far beyond the concrete referent to touch all kinds of experience. The meaning of the metaphor is determined not only by what is there but by what we bring to it out of our experience and out of our imagination. The work of prayer is to fully explore and exploit the metaphor in terms of our own experience. Thus "table" does not mean simply what the speaker in Psalm 23 means, but it means all the good tables at which you have ever sat, the experiences of joy that happened there, and the subsequent vibrations you have from them. "Tears night and day" does not refer simply to the crying a particular psalmist did, but to all the times of crying in the death of the old world; all the times you needed to cry but were unable to; all the bitterness and rejection that both caused and prevented crying. All of that is brought to the metaphor. Metaphors are not packaged announcements; they are receptive vehicles waiting for a whole world of experience that is waiting to come to expression. And if in the praying of the Psalms, we do not bring the dynamic of our own experience, we shall have flat, empty prayers, treating the language as one-dimensional description.

Second, this exposition assumes something about how we read and study and hear these materials. The Psalms do not insist that we follow word for word and line by line, but they intend us to have great freedom to engage our imagination toward the holy God. Our listening mostly moves in and out by a free association of ideas. Whether we plan it or not, are permitted or not, we will take liberties as the psalm passes by to move out into the richness of our experience and then back into the awesome presence of God. That is the way of metaphors. They are not aisles down which we must move; they are more like rockets that explode in ways we cannot predict, causing some things to become unglued and creating new configurations of sensitivity. If we are attentive, the metaphors, like other rockets, may both shatter and illuminate. The Psalms are our partners in prayer. Such evocative language permits each partner a marvelous freedom with which to surprise the other.

Third, I have offered three pairs of metaphors that I suggest can be useful in bringing experience to the Psalms:

- *enemies who destroy / king who orders and governs*
- *tears / table*
- *being trampled / clapping*

The first element of each pair comes from the laments. The speech and experience of disorientation is a sense of being destroyed and trampled, which reduces to tears. The second element in each metaphor of the triad is for celebration: of having a sense of all-rightness, of needing to dramatize it, and of knowing nourishment. With such a simple scheme, many Psalms are embraced, and much of our experience is submitted.

The images and metaphors I have suggested are rather at random. The Psalms are rich with others. If these are not the ones that permit linkage for you, it will be easy enough to find others. If we do our proper work, we will discover that these poetic pilgrimages are indeed ones with God "from whom no secret can be hid." In any case, this kind of language is not flat, obvious, or easy. It is language that requires us to work to bring something of our own experience to it. But it also gives freedom. And when we speak this way, we are surprised by gifts given and lives raised from death.

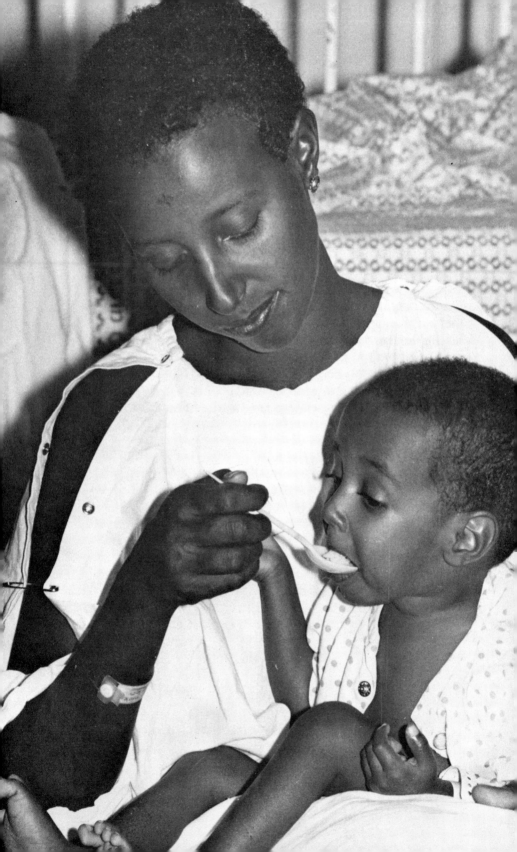

3

Language Appropriate
to a Place

In chapter two, we referred to "the liberation of language." That is the theme we intend to pursue here. It is our argument that the linkage between the Psalms and our experience requires understanding of and attention to language. The movement and meeting of God with us is indeed a speech-event that evokes new humanness among us. Being attentive to language means cultivating the candid imagination to bring our own experience to the Psalms and permitting the speech of the Psalms to discipline it. Conversely, it means letting the Psalms address us and having that language reshape our sensitivities and fill our minds with new pictures and images that may redirect our life.

The notion of the "liberation of language" cuts two ways. On the one hand, we may be more free with our language—to let our language be liberated, not by being permissive or vulgar but by letting it move beyond descriptive functions to evocative, creative functions in our life. That language should be free means we will turn it loose to form new possibilities for us—allowing us to engage in speech that is hope-filled.

On the other hand, the liberation of language is not only about *free speech,* but about *speech freeing us*. When speech is free from a need for exactitude and permitted to reshape our existence and experience, we will encounter new freedom that is more than just freedom of speech, but freedom for faith. Language matters enormously. If our speech and the speech of the Bible must be too closely managed, it likely will restrict both God and us. On the other hand, free speech for God may release the energy that leads to "all things new."

The psalmic metaphors we consider offer to us not descriptions of old situations but *new movements* of God that will change things. Praying the Psalms means being open to God's pilgrimage toward us.

Our work in praying the Psalms is somehow to bring the stylized, disciplined speech of the Psalms together with the raw, ragged, mostly formless experience in our life. We have suggested that a way to do this is by exploration and exploitation of metaphors, that is, words that have concrete reference but that are open to remarkable stretching in many directions in order to touch our experience. The liberation of language means, then, that these words are free to work in many directions, but always without losing contact with their initial concreteness. And as words are used with such freedom, they function evocatively to shape and power our experience in new ways.

Being "In Place" and Displaced

I want now to focus on one specific pair of metaphors that speak of *place*. Paul Tournier has characterized the language of disorientation and reorientation in terms of *finding* one's place and *leaving* one's place for another.[1] The drama of disorientation and reorientation is as old in the Bible as the call to Abraham and Sarah to leave their place and go to another (Gen. 12:1). It is as pertinent as Jesus' calling the disciples to leave everything and to follow him (Mark 1:16–20; 10:28).

I do not suggest that these particular metaphors and images are any more important than others. But I pursue them as suggestive of the imaginative work of linkage that must be done in the praying of the Psalms.

The image of place in the Psalms suggests that in different places one prays different prayers. There are specific kinds of language appropriate to one's situation. Speech about place is speech that enables both parties, speaker and God, to be clear about the nature of the interaction. The well-known Shaker song has it,

> 'Tis a gift to be simple,
> 'tis a gift to be free,

'tis a gift to come down
where you ought to be.

We shall explore two images of place—one that finds Israel in the utterly wrong place, the other that finds Israel finally where it ought to be.

The "Pit" as the Wrong Place

The speech of the wrong place is, of course, found in the prayers of disorientation. In the laments, there is a great deal of talk about the *pit*. First, we know that the pit has concrete reality as a place in which to put people to render them null and void. In the pit, people are effectively removed from life. Historically, this is the device used for Joseph by his brothers (Gen. 37:22,28) and for the prophet Jeremiah by his enemies (Jer. 38:6-9). The pit is used against enemies. It means to deny to a person all the resources necessary for life. It is therefore not difficult to see how the specific reference became an embracive symbol for death. The pit reduces one to powerlessness.

It is of course difficult in the Psalms, as in any powerful poetry, to know when a word is being used descriptively and when it is being used metaphorically. But that is the power of this language. It can always have both tendencies. It is probable that even the speaker was not always clear which way the words should be taken. That is why we may return again and again to these words. Each time we bring something different. And each time we find the Psalms' words shaped and nuanced in fresh ways.

Thus the pit refers to the experience of being rendered powerless. In Psalm 28:1, to "be like those who go down to the Pit," means to be silent, forgotten, dead. This is clearly a cry of disorientation, for the speaker fears losing the old relation with Yahweh, knowing then that everything is lost. In Psalm 88, the language is fuller. The speaker is characterized (verses 4-5) as having no strength and as being forsaken, slain, not remembered, cut off, among the dead. The image evokes a torrent of words. The image is repeated in verse 6, expressed as dark and deep; and in verse 7, we find reference to the flood waters of chaos that will overwhelm. Thus the image tends to slide easily over into another one. If we were to use psychological language in the consideration of this psalm, perhaps we would regard this as "severe depression." But the imagery cuts underneath psychology to talk about the multifaceted experience involved. The poets are powerful in bringing such a struggle to visibility and concreteness. Notice that even though there is great detail, one cannot determine from the psalm what the actual problem is—whether sickness, abandonment, guilt, imprisonment. The poet has an amazing capacity to say much and yet leave everything open. Thus the psalm provides a marvelous receptacle that we are free to fill with our particular experience.

A different word, but one with the same effect, is used in Ps. 30:9, which asserts that the pit is a place so cut off from God that God may neither help nor be praised there. In 35:7, there is a statement of attack against enemies who prepared the pit, so that dislocation may bring about a turning to God not only for vindication but for vengeance.

The cry for vengeance is a powerful part of disorientation. Such a cry blames those who have disrupted and demolished the old equilibrium. Thus in addition to the yearning to be *saved from* the pit, there is the countertheme of wishing others would be *sent there*. There is nothing pious or "Christian" about this prayer. But as psychotherapists know, our deep disorientation is not a time when we are able to be genuinely humane toward others, because we are singularly attentive to the lack of humanness in our own life.

Thus there is the wish that those who have created the pit should be in it (9:15, cf. 94:13). In addition to the concrete word for *pit,* there is use of the word *Sheol.* This word has been mistakenly translated "hell." It does not refer to anything like that, for classical Israelite thought did not envision a place of ultimate punishment. Rather, the term refers simply to a place of undifferentiated, powerless, gray existence where one is removed from joy and discourse with God. There is the wish that the troublemakers should go there (31:17; 55:17; 141:7).

Most remarkably, the dark, discouraging, deathly image of the pit (cistern, ruin, Sheol) is used not only to describe a hopeless situation but also to offer a counterwish of the same for one's enemies. The image also suggests real movement in its use. Those who stay with the image are able to speak not only in *prospect* of the pit or in the *midst* of trouble but also *after* the trouble, in a mood of joy. The image occurs not only in songs of disorientation but also in psalms of thanksgiving that sing of reorientation:

> O LORD, you brought up my soul from *Sheol,*
> > restored me to life from among those gone down to
> > > the *Pit.*
>
> > > > > > > (30:3)

> He drew me up from the desolate *pit,*
> > out of the *miry bog.* . . .
>
> > > > > > > (40:2)

> For you do not give me up to *Sheol,*
> > or let your faithful one see the *Pit.*
>
> > > > > > > (16:10)

> . . . You have delivered my soul from the *depths of Sheol.*
> > > > > > > (86:13)

We may note one other use that is of interest. The same motif is used in the song of thanksgiving in Jon. 2:2. In that context, the reference purports to refer to the experience in the fish, but clearly the psalm itself has an independent existence. Thus the examples of Sheol and pit can be filled with various content, depending on the circumstance of the speaker.

It is clear that the metaphor reports movement: first the cry of *anguish* about the pit; second, the cry of *vengeance;* and third, the voice of *thanksgiving.* The image permits the speaker to stay with the experience and see it through. The motif of pit enables the speaker to present every posture of life to God. Clearly the metaphor of pit in itself is of no interest to the Psalms, but it is a way to bring life to God and have it dealt with.

So we have considered the concrete and metaphorical uses of the pit. Now, third, it remains that the contemporary user of the Psalms should take the image of pit and locate those experiences and dimensions in his or her own life that are "the pits."

This may include being powerless, abandoned, forgotten, lonely, helpless, cheated. It may be something as concrete as remembering "standing in the corner" at school. Or it may be as powerful as a black man being made to "stay in his place," or a woman oppressed by finding her only place to be the kitchen. Such occurrences in our life can, with the help of the Psalms, be given concrete expression, and we can begin the process of moving past them—perhaps even to a song of celebration and thanksgiving. These psalms attest that a life of faith does not protect us from the pit. Rather, the power of God brings us out of the pit to new life, which is not the same as prepit existence. When one is in the pit, one cannot believe or imagine that good can come again. For that reason, the psalmist finally focuses not on the pit but on the One who rules there and everywhere. It is the reality of God that makes clear that the pit is not the place "where you ought to be."

Under Safe Wings

Let us consider, in an abrupt transition, a second figure for place that is in every way contrasted with the first. A favorite image of Israel for a safe place with God is to speak of being under the protective wings of God. Whereas *pit* speaks of danger and threat, *wings* speaks of safety, tenderness, and nurture. There is no doubt that the image is consciously derived from the observation that little birds are safe under the protective wing of the mother hen (cf. Deut. 32:11; Matt. 23:37; Luke 13:34).

But obviously the concrete reference becomes a metaphor that is much used in the songs of lament. It is a figure that yearns for safety, well-being, communion with God, or—in our language—a new orientation.

> Guard me as the apple of the eye;
>> hide me in the *shadow of your wings.*
>
>> (Ps. 17:8)

> Be merciful to me, O God . . .
>> for in you my soul takes refuge;
>> in the *shadow of your wings* I will take refuge. . . .
>
>> (Ps. 57:1)

Now it may occur to some that this is an image of dependency in which one engages in a religious cop-out from the realities of life. That is one possible reading. But the image does not need to be understood as escapism. It may rather be discerned as evangelical realism, acknowledging that the resources for life are not found in us but will have to come from another source outside of self. It is the recognition of the disoriented person that a new orientation must come as a gift. Thus the metaphor embodies an openness to a new purpose, a submission to the will of another, a complete reliance upon someone else's protective concern.

The two images, *protective wing* and *refuge* (which is from the genre of fortress and thus a war image) occur together in the lament of Ps. 61:2*a*–4:

> Lead me to the *rock*
>> that is higher than I;
> for you are my *refuge,*
>> a *strong tower* against the enemy.
> Let me abide in your *tent* for ever,
>> find refuge under the *shelter of your wings.*

Notice here the cluster of images to which are added tent, rock, and tower, used together to contrast with the current situation of need.

As with pit, so these images are not confined to situations of distress. Therefore they occur not only in the laments but also in speeches of confidence and trust, as conclusions drawn from long experience. These are the voices of the reoriented:

> . . . All people may take *refuge* in the *shadow of your*
>> *wings.*
>
> (36:7)

> You would confound the plans of the poor,
>> but the LORD is their *refuge.*
>
> (14:6; cf. 46:1)

These statements have the effect of vetoing the claim of the pit, of denying the pit the capacity to terrorize completely. They assert not that God will be or has promised to be a refuge, but that God *is* a refuge right in the present circumstance. The words

serve to redefine radically the place of the pray-er. He or she is
verbally transported from the *pit* to the *wing,* from the *place of
powerlessness* to *utter safety,* that is, from *death* to *life.* And this
change happens in the bold, free play of evocative language.

Our two positive images occur together in a remarkable
psalm of trust:

> You who live in the *shelter* of the Most High,
>   who abide in the shadow of the Almighty,
> will say to the LORD, "My *refuge* and my fortress;
>   my God, in whom I trust." . . .
> Because you have made the LORD your refuge . . .
> no evil shall befall you. . . .
>
> > (91:1-2,9)

The capacity to speak the Psalms in the full freedom of
imagination is already the embrace of a new orientation, an entry into the kingdom of God. It is of course possible that the
words outdistance the realities. They could be spoken when an
observer might conclude that the person is still, in fact, in the
pit. But we live in pursuit of our imagination. Thus the use of the
psalms of trust while still in the pit is an act of profound hope
that permits new life. Expressing one's trust in God's sheltering
wings is a bold assertion that the power of the pit has been broken. Imaginative speech may outdistance actual circumstance.
But it is a first gesture of transformed circumstance.

Psalm 91 is a remarkable convergence of motifs. In addition
to our two images, it offers a variety of war images (verses 4-8)
that can be usefully explored and exploited. It offers animal imagery in verse 13 and speaks in verse 11 that marvelous offer,
"He will command his angels concerning you." It concludes in
verses 14-16 with one of those rare responses of God that utterly transforms. The self-assertion of God is a response to the boldness of submission:

> . . . I will deliver. . . .
>   I will protect. . . .
> I will answer. . . .
>   I will be with. . . .
>   I will rescue . . . and honor. . . .
> I will satisfy . . . and show. . . .

Finally concerning this metaphor, we should mention its surprising use in Ruth 2:12, where it is used in a narrative. Here, in communication on a human plane, the same image transforms a social situation.

In the Move from Pit to Wing

Our life always moves between the *pit* and the *wing,* between the shattering of disorientation and the gift of life. That is what our baptism is about, to die and to rise with him to newness of life (Rom. 6:1-11).

It remains for the user of this metaphor, like every other, to identify those events and experiences in which hovering wings have cared, in which we have been made utterly safe and so free that life has begun again. Every man, woman, and child has been within and shall again face the pit, and this must be brought to speech. Every one of us has the wings assured to us (cf. Deut. 33:27), and that also must be spoken about.

It is clear that the Psalms, when we freely engage ourselves with them, are indeed subversive literature. They break things loose. They disrupt and question. Most of all, they give us new eyes to see and new tongues to speak. Therefore we need not enter the presence of the Holy One mute and immobilized. We go there to practice our vocation of receiving the new future God is speaking of to us. To risk such prayer is to repent of the old orientation to which we no longer belong. It is to refuse to remain in the pit—which must first be fully experienced—for the sake of the wings, which may be boldly anticipated.

4

Christians in "Jewish Territory"

The Psalms are a centerpiece of Christian liturgy, piety, and spirituality. They have been so from the beginning of the Christian movement for good reason. They have been found poignant in expression, able to empower believing imagination in remarkable ways. This is evident in the rich use made of the Psalms throughout the Christian Testament, most especially in the Passion of Jesus. But the use of the Psalms by Christians is not without awkwardness, for the Psalms are relentlessly Jewish in their mode of expression and in their faith claims. And with our best intent for generosity and good faith, the different nuances of Jewish and Christian faith are not to be overlooked or easily accommodated.

Christian Modes of Avoidance

Two characteristic ways of handling this issue in the Psalms are easily identifiable. The first way is to be *highly selective* and make use of those psalms that are most congenial to us and that contain the least objectionable "Jewishness." We may do this by completely avoiding some psalms—for example, Psalm 109, because it is too full of rancor and venom, or Psalm 137, which too harshly expresses its passion for brutal retaliation. These, it would seem at first glance, have no acceptable place in "conventional Christian faith." Or we may make our selection more delicately and only screen out certain verses. Thus for example, in Psalm 145, a marvelous statement of trust, verse 20*b* comes as a shattering negative at the end and is usually left off. Psalm 95:1-7*a* is a much used call to worship. But verses 7*b*-11 are judged excessively concrete and negative—even though the writer of Heb. 3:7-11, 4:3-11 found these verses pertinent in an appeal for Christian fidelity. We may make our selections on grounds other than those used by the Christian Testament.

But note, we have spoken about "conventional Christian faith." There is, to be sure, a broad body of the Psalms that is not objectionable in this regard. These psalms move in a much broader, more irenic pattern of rhetoric. They speak in a way that lends itself to any serious religious commitment without being excessively concrete. Sensitivity to "Jewish awkwardness" has led much of Christian practice to stay on this "safe" ground. But obviously that is only to avoid, not confront, the question we seek to face here.

The other characteristic way of handling the "Jewishness" of the Psalms (related to the first way) is to claim that Christianity, especially the Christian Testament, evolved from and is superior to the Hebrew Scriptures' Jewishness and thus *supersedes* it and can disregard "objectionable parts." On the one hand, this may lead us to imagine Christians have outgrown the "offensive" Jewishness of the Psalms and so legitimate the criteria for selectivity noted above. On the other hand, Jewish motifs are retained but "spiritualized." That is, they are taken to refer to matters other than the concrete referent. This may permit christological interpretation. This is especially true in reference to "Jerusalem" or "Zion" (cf. 84:7; 122:6; 147:2). These terms may be taken to refer to Jesus, to a heavenly Jerusalem, or, less concretely, to any place of worship or meaning.

Again, a long-standing practice (going back to very early Christian interpretation) is to treat the Psalms as claims about Jesus Christ. In the tradition of Augustine, for example, there is a tendency to find hints about the life, ministry, death, and Resurrection of Jesus at many points in the Psalms.

It is not easy to know how to assess such a practice. It may seem to make the Psalms more readily available for Christian use. Alternatively, however, I suggest such "spiritualizing" tends to tone the Psalms down and avoid the abrasive and offensive elements. On balance, I believe it more helpful to avoid such a practice. We will be helped to a more genuine piety and a more authentic faith if we engage the Psalms as poetry about our common, particular humanness. Nothing should be done that detracts from that reality. Facing such a "Christian" alternative, we should be more attentive to the rawness of Jewish faith out of which the Psalms speak.

But there is yet another alternative. It is in the prayers of Jesus that we may link Jewish ways of praying and christological interpretation. For the prayers of Jesus are surely prayers of a Jew. He prayed as a Jew. The entire tradition of Christian prayer and Christian use of the Psalms must be seen in this light. This gives us warrant for christological interpretation, but the centrality of Jesus can never be far separated from the Jewish character of the material.

We are now, especially because of the Holocaust, at a new place in Jewish-Christian conversations. Old presuppositions and behaviors will no longer do. We are at a new place where we must take each other with a new kind of seriousness, albeit with a new kind of awkwardness. It is clear that either *selectivity* or *spiritualizing* simply avoids the resilient Jewishness of the Psalms. Moreover, our new situation makes clear that something urgent is at stake for Christians in this question. It is clear that the embrace of Jewishness in the Psalter must be faced not for the sake of the Jews, not out of respect because we are "persons of good will," not out of a notion of kinship, but because our spirituality is diminished and trivialized if we neglect the Jewishness that belongs to our own tradition and practice of faith. It is for *our* sake and not the sake of the Jews that we are pressed to make this dimension of the Psalms our own. This is an exceedingly difficult and complex issue, not to be resolved here. Perhaps a discussion of three aspects of the problem can provide a beginning both for our common prayer and for our educational tasks.

Praying for Jews

The Jewishness of the Psalms invites us to pray *for* the Jews. This is not meant to be a condescension, as though our prayers matter more than theirs. Nor does it mean praying for conversion of the Jews—the commonness of our faith precludes any such issue. Rather, it means to bring to utterance the deepest long-ings, echoes, and yearnings of the Jews, for Jews are a paradigm of the deepest longings and yearnings of all of humanity. And we dare say that in them we may hear even the profound sighs of the Almighty; something very Jewish must be practiced in the Almighty's day-to-day sojourn.

For every brand of Jewishness (Zionist or not), these aches and yearnings have to do with Jerusalem. (See Luke 13:34-35; 19:41-44, where Jesus aches and groans over Jerusalem.) In the matrix of the Holocaust and the modern state of Israel, both pre-sent yearnings and future hopes, as well as remembered an-guishes, are linked to Jerusalem.

To pray for Jews is to recognize how pervasive passion for Zion is in the Psalms. Externally, this may be so because the com-pleted Psalter was undoubtedly shaped by priestly or political in-terests for whom Jerusalem is the center of the universe. Thus the Jerusalem interest has a tinge of ideology in the Psalms. It is true that Jerusalem has emerged as a gathering and focusing sym-bol for all of Israel's life. It embodies the memory of great politi-cal power under David and Solomon. It articulates the assurance of God's presence near creation and among humankind (Isa. 4:2-6). It holds the promise of a world of justice and peace (Isa. 2:2-4). As Christians sing with another referent, so Jews may and must sing of Jerusalem.

"The hopes and fears of all the years are met in thee tonight." That carol which sings "tonight" is not very different from the formula from the night of the Passover, which sings of "next year in Jerusalem"—the Jewish rendition of the biblical dream of justice, freedom, and well-being.

Thus after the entry into the Psalter by way of the Torah in Psalm 1, the Psalter moves to Zion in 2:6 and concludes at Zion in 149:2. With the Jews, we can pray for the peace of Jerusalem (122:6). With the Jews, we may set Jerusalem above our highest joy (137:6). With the Jews, we are summoned to praise the Lord (147:12). Indeed, Ps. 128:5 suggests that Jerusalem is always on the tip of the tongue, even when the agenda is something else (cf. 2:6; 122:6; 147:12; 149:2). To be sure, we may know that *in the end time,* true worship is not "placed," but is "in spirit and truth" (John 4:20-24). But *in the meantime* . . .

So there is a tension. We cannot leave Jerusalem as the flat, one-dimensional city of cynical Solomon. But also, we cannot run away from Jerusalem, for it embodies the meanings and the hopes, the fears and the yearnings, of our faith tradition. And we know that it also embodies the best yearnings of most of humanity. The reality of Jerusalem keeps alive among us the conviction that the world is not closed and fixed. Something more is promised. And for that we wait. Praying for Jews means the practice of a solidarity in concrete hope that is old and deep in our faith.

Praying with Jews

Once we have prayed *for* Jews, by turning to Jewish shapes of reality, then we may, perchance, in our use of the Psalms, pray *with* Jews. Our prayer life is always sorely tempted to individualism, or at least to parochialism. God's spirit urges us to pray *alongside*, and so to be genuinely ecumenical. As we pray the Psalms, it is appropriate to ask *which* Jews have used these same Psalms with passion and risk. A parade of victims comes to our imagination. Or, with more immediacy, we may ask which Jews *now* pray these Psalms, from the frightened victims of anti-Semitism to the fated soldiers in the Israeli army, to the Jews in our own culture who are forever displaced and always at the brink of rejection and despisement. To pray with Jews is to be aware of the solidarity with the chosen of God whom the world rejects. To be sure, the Jews are an enigma, and we cannot ever identify that people by any simple category. But they remain as a testimony that God stands by and with and for those whom the world rejects.

To pray *with* introduces a fresh agenda into our Christian spirituality:

1. It tilts us toward a very specific history as *our history*. See, for example, Psalms 78, 105, 106, and 136, which provide a history of betrayal and disobedience, of surprise and deliverance. That history, which becomes ours in prayer, is a minority history, a history of victims and marginalized people. But we need not romanticize. This history is also a memory of grasping and not trusting and thereby bringing trouble. This history may be a critique of our usual histories, on which we count too heavily; a history of a triumphal church or an imperial nation or an intolerant culture. Praying *with* may lead us to another, converted identity.

2. Jews cannot pray very long without meditating on *the Torah* (Psalms 1, 19, 119). The Torah, at the center of spirituality, may deliver us from excessive romanticism or mysticism or subjectivity. Jewish preoccupation with the Torah is hard-nosed realism about the given norms of our life, about the ethical context of our faith, about the public character of true religion. The Torah, at the center, reminds us that the primal mode of faithfulness and knowledge of God is obedience. These Jewish prayers are affirming and joyous, celebrative of the realization that the Torah is not only command but assurance, not only a rule but a bulwark. Reality is structured in ways that will not be defeated. And power is given to share in this God-ordained structuring of reality. Life has a moral coherence on which we can rely. That moral coherence—experienced as obedience—makes a difference to the keeping of God's promises.

3. To pray with Jews means to live with them in the hope and danger of *real judgment.* There is no doubt in the Psalter that God takes folks seriously. On the one hand, God lets us have what we choose (Pss. 1:4-6, 2:7, 50:16-18, 145:20). But on the other hand, the arena for spirituality is this: Jews know that this God who honors our ways is the same God who overrides our ways (Pss. 19:12-13, 103:8-14, 130:3-5). This tension—that God gives us permission to choose our futures and, at the same time, God chooses a future for us that is gracious beyond our choosing—lies at the heart of spirituality in the Psalms. This tension must be lived with and not resolved. It must not be reduced to a scholastic problem of freedom and predestination. In each psalm, each moment must be taken for itself and not yielded easily to some alternative claim or to some overarching scheme. The Jewish awkwardness with which we must contend concerns a special history as the elect ones, a special claim in the Torah that assumes and compels, and a special awe before the reality of God's judgment and mercy. To pray *with* Jews means to stay as long as these poems do at the raw edge with a live God who will not let us settle easily or for too long. There is a precariousness in this life of faith. Jews have known that for a very long time. Such prayer is risky because we are in relation here with a God who is as precarious and at risk as we are. The gift of the Jews in this literature is that we may be engaged with this very same God.

Praying as Jews

If we could genuinely pray *for* Jews and pray *with* Jews, then perhaps we can risk the presumption of praying *as* Jews. (It is of course an enormously presumptuous thing for a Gentile to suggest, but we must not lose nerve in receiving the gift of these texts.) In the providence of God, we might be permitted (and required) to pray *as* Jews. I state the point with two kinds of uneasiness. First, it is impossible to identify Jewishness, and so it is too bold to say what it is to be "as Jews." Second, becoming a Jew takes many centuries and many generations. I am under no romantic illusions about quick transformations. Few of us have lamented in Babylon or been close enough to the ovens when they have been heated. But given those admissions and misgivings, let us hint at five dimensions of Jewishness that mark the Psalms, dimensions that might matter to our spirituality.

I make no claim that these marks are essentially "Jewish." But I speak of them this way on two grounds. First, they seem to me to be the facets of the Psalms that are most troublesome for us, that Christians most prefer to screen out as awkward and offensive. Second, even if they are not definitely Jewish, they at least stand in contrast to the dominant "Greek" reasonableness and idealism that have shaped our spirituality. What I have called "Jewish" at least contrasts with the cool, detached serenity (not to say apathy) of which we are inheritors and too often practitioners.

1. The Psalms are awkward in their *concreteness*. They do not engage in sweeping generalizations to which we are observers. The imagery and speech are pointed and specific. This is true of the historical references to Zion, to kings, to enemies. Psalmic rhetoric is concrete about commandments and punishments, about angers, loves, and hopes. Such a way of prayer may

be a trouble when we want to pray "in general" without focusing anywhere. The "cultural despisers" of biblical faith consistently want a generalized religious consciousness and are offended by God becoming concrete. In Israel, this scandal is in God's way with the "nobodies." In the Christian Testament, the same scandal is in Jesus of Nazareth (Luke 7:22–23). The Psalms are "embodied" prayers.

2. There is little or no slippage between what is thought and felt and what is said. The Psalms are *immediate*. There is no mediation to "clean up," censor, or filter what is going on. This directness reflects a readiness to risk in an uncalculating way with this one "from whom no secret can be hid." The Psalms dare to affirm that since there are no secrets hidden from God, there is less self-deception at work in these prayers. These prayers are marked by candor and robustness with the God who "searches the heart" (Jer. 17:10; Prov. 20:27). These are the prayers of the liberated, who in their freedom are able to speak in an artistic way without ornamentation. Liberated prayer of this kind is filled with passion, with the conviction that in these words, something is at issue that can be resolved in more than one way. And which of the ways of resolution is used depends on how the prayer engages the person of God. The Psalms contain little evidence of depression, either psychological or spiritual. There are active passions such as rage, anger, and hatred, but these are contrasted with the immobility of depression. These psalms in their candor are, on the one hand, sung because the singers have been liberated. On the other hand, these very songs are an act of emancipation. The songs both reflect and accomplish liberation. (It is no wonder that the therapeutic tradition of emancipation grows from this resilient and bold Jewish vision.) In the language of R. D. Laing, there is no split here between "experience" and "behavior."[1] What Israel experiences in the struggle of faith is what it speaks in its behavior of the Psalms. In this identity of thought, feeling, and speech, the Psalms overcome the calculating and careful distance that very much characterizes "polite" piety. Prayer stays very close to the realities of life in these poems.

3. The robustness and candor of the Psalms are especially evident in the *articulation of hatred and anger.* There is no thought here that Israel must be on good behavior in the presence of God. Everything at work in life is readily brought to expression. This prayer is an expression of "no more Mr. Nice Guy." Perhaps this freedom is birthed in the Exodus event, in which Israel knows early that Pharaoh first must be identified as the enemy and then must be verbally assaulted. There is no courteous yearning for reconciliation here. Life is known to be conflicted. And therefore, the practice of conflicted and conflicting speech is necessary. Israel at prayer is ready to carry on linguistic assault against its enemies, one of whom is sometimes God. (Thus, it is not unimportant that the name of Job, that most honest of pray-ers in Israel, means "enemy.") Israel at prayer is prepared to speak as enemy. Israel does not envision a false community in which unequal partners love each other in their unjust and unequal positions.

Well before Paul (Eph. 4:26), the Psalmists endorse the notion, "be angry but do not sin" (cf. Ps. 4:4). Anger is here in abundance. And anger is topped by hatred. The true believer hates powerfully and finds a community with Yahweh (the God of Israel) who also hates:

> Do I not hate those who hate you, O LORD?
> And do I not loathe those who rise up against you?
> I hate them with perfect hatred;
> I count them my enemies.
>
> (Ps. 139:21–22)

Indeed, the speaker, like Yahweh, is never passive or apathetic. Of course it might be objected that the speaker's own hatred is too readily identified with that of God. Perhaps so. But in the moment of hatred, that is what happens to all of us. This anger is not only spiritually liberated; it is psychologically honest. It asserts what each of us, in our moments of insane hatred, tends to do. In that moment, we are incapable of maintaining critical distance from our own sensitivities.

God as well is one who is capable of hatred for evildoers (Ps. 5:5). Our objection to the Psalms' expression of hatred reflects our notion that God is incapable of such a posture. But that is how it is with the God of the Psalms. Such a conviction about God permits this practice of piety.

The rage goes even deeper. The rage born of anger and hatred can be turned against God. In a no-holds-barred extremity,
Job articulates venom even against God:

> Though I am innocent, my own mouth would condemn me;
>   though I am blameless, he would prove me
>   perverse. . . .
> It is all one; therefore I say,
>   he destroys both the blameless
>   and the wicked.
>
> (Job 9:20,22)

There is something peculiarly Jewish about such a posture
that completely reidentifies both God and the speaker. Here is no
"Unmoved Mover," no object to be adored, no "Ground of Being."
Here is the Ultimate Partner, who must enter the fray and be at issue along with the speaker. It should be clear that the Jewish interaction between the two, God and pray-er, is contrasted with
our conventional piety. And we learn so slowly that such candid
piety makes a genuine, healing difference in life. As such, it
serves as an important model for human interaction as well.

4. But Israel is not only able to rage with abandon; it has
equal *passion for hope.* Elie Weisel, that most remarkable story-
teller from the Holocaust, has said that what makes a Jew a Jew
is this inability to quit hoping. Jewishness consists in "going on,"
in persisting, in hoping. Whatever the psychological elements of
hope, the structure of hope is the conviction of a new world. A
new gift from God is at work on our behalf. And this new gift
from God is critiquing, dismantling, and transforming the present age, which is so characterized by injustice and enmity. It is
characteristically Jewish to hope for newness from God, from
this *specific* God who is a giver of newness. Here is no fascina-
tion with "being." Even "nature" is understood as creation, called
by God to bring forth newness (cf. Pss. 65:9–13; 145:13b–16). It
will not do (as Westermann[2] and Terrien[3] have shown) to focus
on historical events to the neglect of the structure and character
of "nature." But "nature" as well (better, "creation") is not fixed
and settled. It also lives under hope and will be transformed for
the new age. Thus Israel hopes for the structures of creation as
well as for the specificity of human communities.

Following Westermann, Gerstenberger has seen that even the lament psalms are acts of hope.[4] They articulate the deepest hurt, anger, and rage of Israel. But they are not statements of resignation that accept the bad situation. Rather, they are insistences upon and expectations from God, who can and will, may and must, keep promises. Many examples could be cited. With two different words, Psalm 71 presents this deep hope:

> For you, O Lord, are my hope,
> my trust, O LORD, from my youth.

(verse 5)

> But I will hope continually,
> and will praise you yet more and more.

(verse 14)

Notice the hope is rooted in God, not in the situation. And hope is affirmed precisely in the face of mocking enemies (verses 10-13).

5. The practice of concreteness and candor, of anger and hope, is carried out with exceeding passion in the Psalms. They prepare us for the most striking and problematic element of Jewish prayer, the *readiness to seek vengeance*. We will delay for now any extended discussion of the topic and take it up separately in the next chapter. For now we must do two things. First, we must recognize that vengeance is both central and problematic in the Psalms. Second, we must recognize that such a yearning for revenge occurs not in a vacuum, but precisely in the context of the qualities we have already presented as characteristically Jewish. The seeking of revenge should be expected from a people who hate and hope with such passion. A religion that practices candor and a piety that is specific will predictably give vent to the yearning for revenge.

As "Jews of Tomorrow"

Notice that these five elements that concern praying *as* Jews provide a critique of much Christian spirituality. Our suggestion is not that we simply observe these factors as interesting items in the Psalms. Rather, the Psalms are an invitation to transform our piety and liturgy in ways that will make both piety and liturgy somewhat risky and certainly abrasive. Lewis Mumford has written of the relentless Jewish resistance to every assimilation.[5] Jewishness, wherever it occurs, is awkward for those who want to create a "universal culture," or a "preachable kingdom." The practice of Jewish piety maintains its odd angularity, an angularity that has dangerous public implications. Obviously a people so passionate in prayer will not willingly practice silent subservience in public life. A community so laden with visions of the Torah will not be silent in the streets about injustice. Prayers *with* and *for* and *as* the people of Jerusalem will not long acquiesce in public violation of these visions.

Finally, a word in anticipation of response to these comments. Surely it will occur to some that such an insistence on Jewishness, and especially Jerusalem, is not very evenhanded toward the current political issues surrounding Israel and Jerusalem. My comments have important political implications, but not of that kind.

The theological claims I have made here for Jewishness cut in various ways concerning historical responsibility and political reality. There is a closed kind of Jewishness that can become politically totalitarian. Such a Jewishness is no doubt at work in the modern world, and no doubt one can find some warrant in the Psalms. But there is another kind of Jewishness in the Psalter. And it is to that alternative Jewishness that attention must be drawn. The tension we face in the Psalms (and everywhere in the Hebrew Scriptures) is the tension between *largeness of vision* and *passion for particularity.* Thus far, we have focused on the passion for particularity because I judge that to be the stumbling block for many Christians who face the Psalms.

But largeness of vision is not antithetical to such a passion for particularity. It grows out of it. The elect people bear witness to an all-inclusive providence. So the countertheme to Jewish particularity is a vision of all peoples who may also be citizens of Jerusalem (cf. Isa. 2:2–4; Rev. 21:1–4) or who may be reckoned as distinct from Israel but nonetheless part of the fulfillment of God's promise (Isa. 19:23–25).

1. The Psalms have a *passion for the righteous,* for the practitioners of God's vision for justice and peace (Pss. 1:5-6; 7:9; 11:7; 34:15; 92:12). And the Psalms are reluctant to equate this commitment with any narrow community. In its largeness of vision, Israel knows there are "Torah keepers" in various communities, some of which bear other names (Isa. 56:6-8).

2. The Psalms have a *passion for the poor and needy* (Pss. 69:33; 109:31; 140:12), for those who are broken of spirit and heart (Pss. 34:18; 51:17). God's compassion is not toward an ethnic community nor those with a pedigree, but toward those in special need.

These elements also belong to the Jewishness of the Psalter. Thus as one envisions the drama of Jerusalem and as those who yearn to be "next year in freedom," the pilgrimage to Jerusalem is a strange procession. That procession toward newness includes the Jews who bear a public identity, but it also includes refugees who are remote from the name "Jew." The Jewishness to which the Psalter calls us is not that of "yesterday's Jews" who rest on the faith of their parents (cf. Matt. 3:9), but on the "Jews of tomorrow" who dare to believe God's concrete promises with passion.

There is a strange restlessness and shattering that belongs to Jewishness. When we learn to pray these prayers faithfully, we shall all be scandalized. Thus I propose that, at the end, conventional notions of Jewishness are also placed in question. But that is only at the end, after we have learned the passion and the patience to pray *for* and *with* and *as* Jews.

5

Vengeance: Human and Divine

The most troublesome dimension of the Psalms is the agenda of vengeance. It may also be the most theologically poignant, as we hope to show. The cry for retaliation at one's enemies at least surprises us. We do not expect to find such a note in "religious" literature. It may offend us, and it does not fit very well in our usual notions of faith, piety, or spirituality. To some extent, we are prepared for it by our recognition (in the last chapter) that the Psalms reflect unabashed concreteness, candor, and passion. The Psalms explore the full gamut of human experience from rage to hope. Indeed, it would be very strange if such a robust spirituality lacked such a dimension of vengeance, for we would conclude that just at the crucial point, robustness had turned to cowardice and propriety. The vitality of the Psalms, if without a hunger for vengeance, would be a cop-out. But we need have no fear of that. There is no such failure of nerve, no backing down from this religion on the brink of stridency. Thus the expression of vengeance is not unnatural, unexpected, or inappropriate. But that in no way diminishes its problematic character.

The Reality of Vengeance

Let us begin with two acts of realism. First, *the yearning for vengeance is there in the Psalms.* It is there, without embarrassment, apology, or censor. Whatever we say on the subject must be linked to that undeniable fact. We are not free to explain it away. If we are genuinely to pray the Psalms, we must try to understand what is happening in such acts of piety. Certainly no expurgated, "selective" version of the Psalms will do. For that is only to push the problem away. Such "selectivity" does not avoid the presence of the motif. Indeed, selective avoidance will cause us to miss the resources that we may find there.

The counterpart, a second act of realism, is that *the yearning for vengeance is here, among us and within us* and with power. It is not only *there* in the Psalms, but it is *here* in the human heart and the human community. When we know ourselves as well as the Psalter knows us, we recognize that we are creatures who wish for vengeance and retaliation. We wish in every way we can to be right and, if not right, at least stronger. Perhaps we do not engage in child abuse or spouse abuse, and we do not urge the death penalty (at least not all of us do). But in lesser ways, we assault verbally or we nurse affronts, waiting for their reversal and satisfaction. It could be that, for some few, these passions are absent or that, for more of us, they are absent on occasion. But we must not be so romantic as to imagine we have outgrown the eagerness for retaliation. While developmental psychology may discern other more positive yearnings as an ideal, theological realism cannot afford such deception. The real theological problem, I submit, is not that vengeance is *there* in the Psalms, but that it is *here* in our midst. And that it is there *and* here only reflects how attuned the Psalter is to what goes on among us. Thus, we may begin with a recognition of the acute correspondence between what is *written there* and what is *practiced here*. The Psalms do "tell it like it is" with us.

So let us begin with such realism about the poetry and about ourselves. The articulation of vengeance leads us to new awarenesses about ourselves. That is, the yearning for vengeance belongs to any serious understanding of human personality. It is important that Psalm 139 celebrates the mystery of human personhood (verses 1–2, 13–15); and the same Psalm expresses the capacity for hatred (verses 21–22). The capacity for hatred belongs to the mystery of personhood.

The Psalms are the rhetorical practice in fullest measure of what is in us. John Calvin describes the Psalms as "An Anatomy of all Parts of the Soul."[1] And so they are. They tell all about us. The Psalms provide space for full linguistic freedom in which nothing is censored or precluded. Thus Psalm 109 surely engages in "overkill" in its wishes and prayers against the "wicked." The words pile up like our nuclear stockpiles, without recognizing that nobody needs to be or could possibly be violated in that many ways. But this is not action. It is words, a flight of passion in imagination.

Such imagination, in which the speaker strains to be vivid and venomous and almost exhibitionist, surely performs several functions:

a. It is no doubt *cathartic*. We need not flinch from the therapeutic value of the Psalms. In our heavily censored society, this is one place left in which it may all be spoken.

b. But it is more than cathartic, more than simply giving expression to what we have felt and known all along. In genuine rage, words do not simply follow feelings. They lead them. It is speech that lets us discover the power, depth, and intensity of the hurt. The Psalms are acts of self-discovery that penetrate the facade of sweet graciousness.

c. The Psalms serve to legitimate and affirm these most intense elements of rage. In such speech, we discover that our words (and feelings) do not destroy the enemy, that is, they are not as dangerous as we thought. Nor do our words bring judgment from heaven on us. The world (or God) is not as censorious as we feared. Such speech puts rage in perspective. Our feelings brought to speech are not as dangerous or as important as we imagined, as we wished, or as we feared. When they are unspoken, they loom too large, and we are condemned by them. When spoken, our intense thoughts and feelings are brought into a context in which they can be discerned differently. Notice that in Psalm 109, after the long recital of rage through verse 19, the intensity is spent. Then the speaker must return to the reality of heart and fear and helplessness in verses 22–25. The rage is a prelude to the real agenda of attitudes about oneself.

It is important to recognize that these verbal assaults of imagination and hyperbole are *verbal*. They speak wishes and prayers. But the speaker doesn't *do* anything beyond speak. The *speech* of vengeance is not to be equated with *acts* of vengeance. This community that respected and greatly valued language encouraged speech, destructive as it might be, in the place of destructive action. So far as we know, even in the most violent cries for vengeance, no action is taken. These Psalms might help us reflect on retaliatory violence in a society that has lost its places and legitimacy for speech. Where there is no valued *speech of assault* for the powerless, the risks of deathly action are much higher from persons in despair.

The speech of vengeance is characteristically offered to God, not directly to the enemy. Thus Psalm 109 begins with an address to God. And in verse 21, the turn from venom to self-reflection happens in, "But Thou" (RSV). The final appeal in verse 26 is no longer an urging to action but an imperative that God should act. That is, vengeance is transferred from the heart of the speaker to the heart of God. The Psalm characteristically is structured to show that vengeance is not simply a psychological but a theological matter. It must be referred to God. And when vengeance is entrusted to God, the speaker is relatively free from its power. The speaker, with all the hurt and joy, affirms himself or herself to be God's creature. That recognition of being in God's realm and able to address God gives perspective to the venom.

Thus the movement of the speech is in two parts. First, the vengeance must be fully recognized as present, fully owned as "my" rage, and fully expressed with as much power and intensity as possible. It must be given freedom for full play and visibility. It is analogous to grief. We know grief is best handled by full articulation. And Israel knows that same thing about rage.

But second, this full rage and bitterness is yielded to God's wisdom and providential care. This happens when the speaker finally says, "But Thou."[2] The yielding cannot be full and free unless the articulation and owning is first full and free. That submission to God is an act of faith and confidence. The speaker has no doubt that God will honor and take seriously the need for vengeance and will act upon that need. But the doxology of Ps. 109:30-31 makes clear that the final confidence is in God. It is not in the rightness of the venom or the legitimacy of the rage. There is no sense of being triumphant, but only of being very sure of God. By the end of such a Psalm, the cry for vengeance is not resolved. The rage is not removed. But it has been dramatically transformed by the double step of *owning* and *yielding*.

God's Vengeance and Our Vengeance

But such a prayer still shocks us. And it drives the issue one step further. *What about God?* What about this God who receives such prayers and at least leaves open the impression that the venom is shared and acted upon. We need to begin by recognizing two things about God's self-presentation in the Psalms and in the entire Bible. First, there is no single, coherent picture of God. Nor is there a neat development from a vengeful to a loving God. Rather, there are various sketches and disclosures in different circumstances. Each such disclosure is offered on its own and makes its own claim. And each such sketch must be fully honored on its own without being reduced to a generalized portrait.

Second, every presentation of God is filtered through human imagination. The God presented in any sketch is not untouched by human interest, human need, and human wish. We can easily see that people with passionate hates assign these same hates to God. That is, we find it easy to identify our passions with the passions of God, and collapse the distance between us and the Holy One. But we must recognize that the "nice" presentations of God—as loving, forgiving, merciful—are also filtered through human interest, human need, and human wish.

So we may not easily take some disclosures of God as "more nearly true" simply because we happen to like them. The mystery, sovereignty, and freedom of God require us to hold loosely even our preferred sketches of God. Nowhere is this more important than in the question of vengeance. In these poems, we have an "interested," theological statement. But such a statement is not made without authenticity. That is, this is *serious* speech addressed to a *real* God, about things *genuinely important.* Our best theological treatment recognizes that these speeches may articulate our most important concerns to God. We take these statements seriously only if we regard them as well-intended and deeply felt prayers.

1. The Psalms (and the entire Bible) are clear that *vengeance belongs to God* (Deut. 32:35; Ps. 94:1; Isa. 63:4; Rom. 12:19; Heb. 10:30). Vengeance is not human business. Now it may trouble us that this God is concerned with vengeance. But we may begin with the awareness that assigning vengeance to God means an end to human vengeance. It is a liberating assertion that I do not need to trouble myself with retaliation, for that is left safely in God's hands. The Psalmist seems to know this, and the venomous words show that the reality of vengeance is present. But that these words are addressed to God shows a recognition that this is God's business and not ours. That is the first and most important thing to say about God's vengeance. To affirm that vengeance belongs to God is an act of profound faith. Conversely, to try to keep some vengeance for oneself and to withhold it from God is to mistrust God, as though we could do it better than God. Affirmation of God's vengeance is in fact a yielding.

2. God's vengeance is understood as *the other side of God's compassion*—the sovereign redress of a wrong. That is, in the Hebrew Scriptures, the two motifs belong together. God cannot act to liberate the chosen people without at the same time judging and punishing the oppressors who have perverted a just ordering of life. Vengeance by God is not understood as an end in itself. It is discerned as necessary to the establishment and preservation of a just rule. It is a way God "right-wises" life. Thus Duet. 32:35 speaks of vengeance. But this is linked in verse 36 with vindication and compassion for God's servants. Such a juxtaposition expresses political realism. When things are shifted on behalf of someone, it means a painful loss for someone else, who has encroached on the claims of the first party. Such a juxtaposition may also reflect some childishness. When we are hurt, we do not feel the situation completely righted by compassion unless the offender is also dealt with. This understanding does not eliminate all the theological problems, but it is helpful to see that vengeance is the dark side, perhaps the inevitably dark side, of the mercy of God. Thus:

> Who struck Egypt through their firstborn,
> > for his steadfast love endures forever . . .
> who struck down great kings,
> > for his steadfast love endures forever.

> (Ps. 136:10,17)

The killing of the firstborn does not sound like "steadfast love," and it was not so perceived by any Egyptian. But that is steadfast love if one is an Israelite. And such an action is necessary to liberate, though from another perspective, it is simply ruthless vengeance.

3. That God practices vengeance is one way the Bible has of speaking about *moral coherence and moral order* in which God is actively engaged. The God of the Bible is never neutral, objective, indifferent, or simply balancing things. The world is not on its own. There is an accountability to the purposes of God to which all must answer. God who saves and creates also watches over the divine will and judges those who violate those purposes. Thus the God who keeps loyalty for thousands is also the one who visits iniquities to the fourth generation (Exod. 34:6-7). God's judgment is especially turned against the "wicked," those who do not serve the sovereign purpose (cf. Ps. 58:10; 149:7). The passionate appeal for faithfulness in the Letter to the Hebrews, chapter 10, ends with such an affirmation:

> For we know the one who said, "Vengeance is mine, I will repay." And again, "The Lord will judge his people." It is a fearful thing to fall into the hands of the living God.
>
> (verses 30-31)

Such heavy imagery may not suit our tastes. But it is the imagery found most compelling in terms of urgency in the church (cf. Luke 21:22). It may surprise some to note these anticipations of vengeance even in the Christian Testament.

4. The reality of juxtaposition (vengeance is the back side of compassion) and the assurance of moral coherence in which God has a stake (i.e., God takes human action seriously in terms of divine purpose) leads to the affirmation that *God has taken sides in history* and acts effectively on behalf of special partners. In the beginning, that special partner is Israel. And so the compassion is for Israel; the vengeance is against the enemies of Israel. That is why there is the balance of the rescue of Israel and the destruction of others, as in Ps. 136:10,15,17-20. But Israel never becomes the possessor of God's compassion, nor the manager of God's vengeance. Both belong peculiarly to God. God alone exercises them in sovereign freedom and for the sake of that sovereign freedom. When Job's friends, for example, imagine they can "administer" God's compassion, they are dismissed as "foolish."

Thus, in the long run the benefactor of God's compassion and vengeance is not Israel in any mechanical way. Rather, God's action is taken on behalf of:

a. the *faithful* (i.e., righteous, obedient), those who keep the Torah:

> The righteous will rejoice when they see vengeance done;
>> they will bathe their feet in the blood of the wicked.
> People will say, "Surely there is a reward for the righteous;
>> surely there is a God who judges on earth."
>>>> (Ps. 58:10-11; cf. Exod. 34:6)

b. the *poor and needy* who are objects of special concern:

> Say to those who are of a fearful heart,
>> "Be strong, do not fear!
> Here is your God.
>> He will come with *vengeance,*
> with terrible recompense.
>> He will come and save you."
>
> Then the eyes of the blind shall be opened,
>> and the ears of the deaf unstopped;
> Then the lame shall leap like a deer,
>> and the tongue of the speechless sing for joy.
>>>> (Isa. 35:4-6)

> . . . to bring good news to the oppressed . . .
> to proclaim liberty to the captives . . .
> to proclaim the year of the LORD's favor,
>> and the day of *vengeance* of our God. . . .
>>>> (Isa. 61:1-2)

> O LORD, you God of *vengeance,*
>> you God of *vengeance,* shine forth! . . .
> O LORD, how long shall the wicked,
>> how long shall the wicked exult? . . .
> They kill the widow and the stranger,
>> and murder the orphan.
>>>> (Ps. 94:1,3,6; cf. 9:18; 12:5-7; 34:6; 35:10)

It is evident that this motif of *vengeance for the poor* is carried into the Christian Testament, especially in the Gospel of Luke. It is articulated in the song of Mary (Luke 1:51-53) and in the inaugural presentation of Jesus (Luke 4:18-19), which quotes Isa. 61:1-2. The day of God's vengeance is the day of reversals[3] for the poor and against the unjust rich.

The vengeance of God is not indiscriminate anger. It is a reflection of God's zeal for justice and freedom. God will not quit until the divine will is accomplished, which is at odds with the ways of the world (cf. Isa. 55:6-9). When God's way is thwarted, say the Psalms, God powerfully intervenes—that is, the God with whom we must deal in this practice of psalmic spirituality.

There is no doubt that many of the uses of the vengeance motif in the Psalms are a mixture of good theology and self-interested plea. The speaker identifies himself or herself as one of the faithful deserving poor who has a right to expect and insist upon God's compassionate and vengeful intervention (cf. Ps. 40:17; 69:29).

This is most poignantly expressed in the "confessions" of Jeremiah. Jeremiah regards himself as undoubtedly one of the faithful poor who asks for compassion, which must come as vengeance (cf. Jer. 11:20, 20:12). With Jeremiah, as with us and with the psalmists, there are no disinterested pray-ers. But the psalmists are bold to see an appropriate linkage between God's primal commitment and our situation of need. God's commitment is invoked because of a situation of distress that God does not will. And so God is summoned to intervene and to invert the situation. It is that appropriate linkage that is expressed in these psalms. Such prayer is offered, but not because of reasoned conclusion. Rather, in the hurt, anger, and shame, the point of contact is, on the one hand, the overwhelming need and, on the other, the awareness that Yahweh, God of Israel, is all we have. In that moment of need, Israel's God is the last, best hope of the believing community. And so Israel must seek rectification,[4] and that requires forceful action.

Vengeance and Compassion

Having said all of that, we may note that this settlement of the question of vengeance is provisional. The most sensitive poets of Israel are troubled about this way of thinking. At peak moments of literary insight and theological imagination, they know God to be troubled too.

In the Hebrew Scriptures, we may cite two texts, parallel in structure, that disclose the struggle in the heart of God. In the flood narrative, beginning in Gen. 6:5-7 God resolves to take vengeance on wayward creation. But note that God makes the resolve not in anger, but in grief and sorrow. The flood narrative spins out the troubled tale. But by 8:21, something decisive has happened. Nothing is changed in the imagination of humankind, which is still evil. What has happened is a change wrought in the heart of God, who will no longer take vengeance. The move in God's heart from 6:5-7 to 8:21 suggests that instead of humankind suffering, God takes the suffering and owns it. God resolves to turn the grief inward rather than to rage against creation. God bears the *vengeance* of God in order that all of creation can have compassion.

The same "turn" is more visible in Hos. 11:1-9. Verses 1-7 are a conventional statement of God's anger and punishment. But in verses 8-9, God has internalized the rage, turned the anger so that even God's own "heart recoils." God resolves not to take vengeance on Israel, but to contain it. In this profound moment, God breaks with the habits of heaven and earth and shows radical graciousness. This is "God and no mortal." This is a God unlike any of the other gods (cf. Psalm 82). Such graciousness is not easy, in heaven or on earth. It is not simply or obviously gained. It is gained only by God's acceptance and internalization of the vengeance that gets outwardly expressed, now, only as compassion. Unmitigated compassion is possible only because God bears the pain of vengeance.

A Way Through Vengeance

Finally we must ask, how does Christian faith assess these statements about the vengeance of God? How are these themes taken up in the Christian Testament? There is some ground for saying that the Christian Testament discloses God as having moved from vengeance to compassion. But that argument must be articulated very delicately:

1. We must not pretend that the Christian Testament gives a "higher" view of God in contrast to the Hebrew Scriptures. Such an evolutionary notion misreads the evidence. In the entire Bible, we have to deal with the same God.

2. We have seen that the Hebrew Scriptures already knows about the problem in the experience of God's vengeance. Israel already understands that the grief of God moves beyond vengeance. In addition to Gen. 6:5-7; 8:20-22; and Hos. 11:8-9, which we have cited, see Pss. 103:6-14 and 130.

3. We have seen that the Christian Testament still makes important use of the motif of God's vengeance. In the Christian Testament, this God has not become a romantic who has no passion for divine purposes. This God still holds to jealous sovereignty and intervenes for the sake of it. There is no way around the hard sayings in the Christian Testament.

4. But, finally, we come to those staggering ethical injunctions about love in the place of *vengeance:*

"You have heard that it was said, 'You shall love your neighbor and hate your enemy.' But I say to you, Love your enemies and pray for those who persecute you, so that you may be children of your Father in heaven; for he makes his sun rise on the evil and on the good, and sends rain on the righteous and on the unrighteous. . . . Be perfect, therefore, as your heavenly Father is perfect."

(Matt. 5:43-48)

Bless those who persecute you; bless and do not curse them. . . . Beloved, never avenge yourselves, but leave room for the wrath of God; for it is written, "Vengeance is mine, I will repay, says the Lord." . . . Do not be overcome by evil, but overcome evil with good.

(Rom. 12:14-21)

This is the most extreme claim made in this regard. But notice, these ethical statements are in fact theological claims. What we are to *do* relates to *who God is:* "Be perfect, as your heavenly Father is perfect." The possibility of a vengeance-free ethic is rooted in the staggering reality of God. And so we are driven to the Crucifixion, in which God has decisively dealt with the reality of evil, which must be judged. God has responded with a powerful inclination for justice. There is no less vengeance in the Christian Testament. But God has wrought it upon God, and so the world has been purged and grace has triumphed.

For those who are troubled about the psalms of vengeance, there is a way beyond them. But that way is not easy or "natural." It is not the way of careless religious goodwill. It is not the way of moral indifference or flippancy. It is, rather, the way of crucifixion, of accepting the rage and grief and terror of evil in ourselves in order to be liberated for compassion toward others. In the Gospel, Christians know "a more excellent way" (1 Cor. 12:31). But it is not the first way. My hunch is that there is a way *beyond* the psalms of vengeance, but it is a way *through* them and not *around* them. And that is so because of what in fact goes on with us. Willy-nilly, we are vengeful creatures. Thus these harsh psalms must be fully embraced as our own. Our rage and indignation must be fully owned and fully expressed. Then (and *only* then) can our rage and indignation be yielded to the mercy of God. In taking this route through the Psalms, we take the route God has gone. We are not permitted a cheaper, easier, more "enlightened" way.[5]

Notes

Chapter 1: Letting Experience Touch the Psalter

1. Peter L. Berger, *A Rumor of Angels* (Garden City, NY: Doubleday and Co., 1969).

2. Langdon Gilkey, *Naming the Whirlwind* (Indianapolis: Bobbs-Merrill Co., 1969).

3. Paul Ricoeur, "Biblical Hermeneutics," *Semeia* 4 (1975): 108–135.

4. Anticipating Ricoeur in important ways, Karl Barth wrote: "It is no accident that of all the books of the Hebrew Scriptures the Psalter has always been found the most relevant. This is not in spite of the fact, but just because of it, that in so many passages it echoes the people of the covenant trembling for its preservation in final extremity before its all-powerful enemies. The Christian community always has good reason to see itself in this people, and to take on its own lips the words of its helpless sighing, the cries which it utters from the depths of its need. It turns to the Psalter, not in spite of the fact, but just because of it, that as the community of Jesus Christ it knows that it is established on the rock (as powerfully attested by the Psalms themselves), but on the rock which, although it is sure and impregnable in itself, is attacked on all sides, and seems to be of very doubtful security in the eyes of all men and therefore in its own." Karl Barth, *Church Dogmatics IV* (Edinburgh, Scotland: T and T Clark, 1958), p. 671.

5. Ernest Becker, *The Denial of Death* (New York: The Free Press, 1973).

6. On the cruciality of thanksgiving for the faith and worship of Israel, see the fine discussion by Harvey Guthrie, *Theology as Thanksgiving* (New York: Seabury Press, 1981).

Chapter 2: The Liberation of Language

1. Paul Ricoeur, *Freud and Philosophy* (New Haven, CT: Yale University Press, 1970), pp. 165-177. Ricoeur increasingly seeks a hermeneutic of anticipation, which draws his work into relation with that of Jürgen Habermas.

2. On the lament as the route to hope, see Erhard Gerstenberger, "Der klagende Mensch," in *Probleme biblischer Theologie,* ed. Hans Walter Wolff (Munich, Germany: Chr. Kaiser Verlag, 1971), pp. 64-72; and Walter Brueggemann, "The Formfulness of Grief," *Interpretation* 31 (1977): 263-275.

Chapter 3: Language Appropriate to a Place

1. Paul Tournier, *A Place for You* (New York: Harper and Row, 1968).

Chapter 4: Christians in "Jewish Territory"

1. R. D. Laing, *The Politics of Experience* (New York: Random House, 1967), especially chapter 1.

2. Claus Westermann has most fully articulated this viewpoint in *What Does the Old Testament Say About God?* (Atlanta: John Knox Press, 1979), especially chapter 3. His earlier succinct statement is, "Creation and History in the Old Testament," in *The Gospel and Human Destiny,* ed. Vilmos Vajta (Minneapolis: Augsburg Publishing House, 1971), pp. 11-38.

3. Samuel Terrien, *The Elusive Presence* (New York: Harper and Row, 1978).

4. See Gerstenberger's work previously cited herein (chapter 2, note 2). For a contemporary explication of this insight, see Erhard Gerstenberger and Wolfgang Schrage, *Suffering* (Nashville, TN: Abingdon Press, 1980), pp. 130-135.

5. Lewis Mumford, *The Myth of the Machine* (New York: Harcourt, Brace and World, 1966, 1967), pp. 232-233.

Chapter 5: Vengeance

1. Stated in his preface to the *Commentary on Psalms*. See Ford Lewis Battles, *The Piety of John Calvin* (Grand Rapids, MI: Baker Book House, 1978), p. 27.

2. Terrien, *The Elusive Presence*, p. 316, observes the function and power of "Thou" in Psalm 73: "An inquisitive essay has become a prayer. The skeptic, who pondered intellectual answers to difficult questions, suddenly addressed the Deity as 'Thou.' He inserted his doubt into the context of his adoration. . . . Therefore, he no longer pursued his trend of thinking within the confines of his autonomous self but pursued it instead in the presence of the Godhead."

3. On the theme of "reversal of fortune," see Norman Gottwald, *The Tribes of Yahweh* (Maryknoll, NY: Orbis Books, 1979), pp. 534–540. His focus is on the Song of Hannah. And that in turn is reflected in the Magnificat of Mary. Gottwald is especially attentive to the way in which reversal, which is a literary-rhetorical event, may be evocative of a political-economic reversal.

4. George Mendenhall, *The Tenth Generation* (Baltimore: Johns Hopkins University Press, 1973), chapter 3, has provided an especially helpful discussion of vengeance. It is his argument that vengeance is a political idea and ought not to be understood as a raw, primitive seeking of retaliation. Rather, it is the maintenance of political order and sovereignty in an established "Imperium." The responsible Lord intervenes to right situations that have departed from the overall governing pattern. Thus vengeance is both punishment and vindication in Israel. While I have not followed Mendenhall precisely, his essay is especially suggestive.

5. Marie Augusta Neal, *A Socio-Theology of Letting Go* (New York: Paulist Press, 1975), discusses the need for "relinquishment" of an economic kind. To be viable, such economic relinquishment must be matched by linguistic, liturgical, emotional "letting go."